MBA
IN A BOOK

Also edited by Leslie Pockell and Adrienne Avila

The 100 Best Poems of All Time

The 100 Best Love Poems of All Time

100 Poems to Lift Your Spirits (with Celia Johnson)

The 13 Best Horror Stories of All Time

Everything I've Learned

The 101 Greatest Business Principles of All Time

The 100 Greatest Sales Tips of All Time

The 100 Greatest Leadership Principles of All Time

Only the Best/Solo lo Mejor

Fundamental Principles of
Business, Sales, and Leadership

MBA

IN A BOOK

EDITED BY
LESLIE POCKELL
WITH ADRIENNE AVILA

**BUSINESS
PLUS**

NEW YORK   BOSTON

Business Plus
Hachette Book Group
237 Park Avenue
New York, NY 10017

Visit our Web site at www.HachetteBookGroup.com

The 101 Greatest Business Principles of All Time, The 100 Greatest Sales Tips of All Time,
and *The 100 Greatest Leadership Principles of All Time* originally published in hardcover
by Hachette Book Group.

Printed in the United States of America

First Compilation Edition: March 2009

10 9 8 7 6 5 4 3 2 1

Business Plus is an imprint of Grand Central Publishing.
The Business Plus name and logo are trademarks of Hachette Book Group, Inc.

LCCN: 2008921448
ISBN 978-0-446-53543-4

Book Design & Composition by Mada Design, Inc.

CONTENTS

◆

INTRODUCTION

◆

The world of business is no place for amateurs, and it usually takes years of running a gauntlet of mistaken assumptions and damaging missteps to become a true professional. The conventional MBA program provides all sorts of terminology and case studies that allow enthusiastic graduates to talk the talk of business, but like military basic training, it is no substitute for the realities of the battlefield. No matter how academically prepared you may feel, you will encounter many obstacles along the way, as did those whose words of wisdom are included here. It is our hope that this book will serve as a kind of reference and guide to essential business, sales, and leadership principles, while occasionally inspiring you as a mentor would, introducing concepts and revealing truths that every businessperson encounters at some time in their career. You may or may not possess an actual master's degree in business administration, but with *MBA in a Book* you will have at your fingertips a handy and reliable guide to everything a successful business leader needs to know.

This volume is an omnibus made up of three earlier works that focused respectively on primary business principles, sales tips, and leadership. The first part, **Business Principles**, includes advice and information on the fundamentals of business, including insights into investment, management, marketing, and the idea of success in general. The second part, **Sales Tips**, covers motivation, preparation, presentation, and service. Finally, the section on **Leadership Principles** addresses the primary elements of leadership, as identified by the Chinese military strategist Sun Tzu: intelligence, trustworthiness, humaneness, courage, and discipline.

It is our hope that readers of this book will keep it handy for use as a kind of Swiss Army knife of business: Whenever a business challenge or question arises, this book should provide the right tool to deal with it successfully.

We'd like to thank Beth DeGuzman, Rick Wolff, and Jamie Raab for their support of this project, and Rebecca Isenberg and Patricia Canseco for their editorial contributions.

Leslie Pockell
Adrienne Avila

PART I:
BUSINESS PRINCIPLES

◆

This section contains concise explications of fundamental business principles that every professional should know, or at least have at their fingertips. This information is derived from the writings of some of the most eminent economic theorists and philosophers of all time, together with distinguished entrepreneurs, managers, investors, and creative geniuses from every era. In addition, some revelatory truths come from more unlikely sources, including the Bible, an advice columnist, and a country singer. To maximize the breadth of the insights provided here, we have included no more than one principle per person.

At first glance, some of the principles included here may seem simplistic rather than profound; others may appear to overlap, or to be contradictory. Still others may appear facetious. But it is our belief that, taken together, they will help to inculcate some basic realities that are valid for both business and life as a whole. The world of business, like the world at large, is not something that is controllable by power, wealth, or force of will alone; while useful guidelines certainly exist, there are no magic formulas. After all, business ultimately involves people, each of whom has needs, desires, strengths, and weaknesses. It is those who are best able to communicate with, empathize with, and inspire their colleagues and their customers, and to mobilize their strengths and minimize their weaknesses, who are most likely to succeed in the world of business.

The Fundamentals

Buy cheap, sell dear.

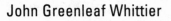

John Greenleaf Whittier

Only a fool holds out for top dollar.

◆

Joseph P. Kennedy

Cut your losses, and let your profits run.

◆

Anonymous

The engine which drives Enterprise
is not Thrift, but Profit.

◆

John Maynard Keynes

There are three secrets to real estate:
Location, location, location.

William Dillard

If you can run one business well,
you can run any business well.

◆

Richard Branson

For unto every one that hath shall be given, and he shall have abundance: but from him that hath not shall be taken away even that which he hath.

Matthew 25:29

Every individual . . . intends only his own gain, and he is in this, as in many other cases, led by an invisible hand to promote an end which was no part of his intention. Nor is it always the worse for the society that it was no part of it. By pursuing his own interest he frequently promotes that of the society more effectually than when he really intends to promote it.

◆

Adam Smith, *The Wealth of Nations*

PARETO'S PRINCIPLE

Twenty percent of your products will
generate eighty percent of your income.
Twenty percent of your income will require
eighty percent of your resources.

◆

Vilfredo Pareto

There was an old owl lived in an oak,
The more he heard, the less he spoke;
The less he spoke, the more he heard.
O, if men were like that wise old bird.

Punch

A dinner lubricates business.

◆

William Scott, Baron Stowell

PARKINSON'S LAW

Work expands so as to fill the time
available for its completion.

C. Northcote Parkinson

THE PETER PRINCIPLE

In a hierarchical organization
every employee tends to rise to
his level of incompetence.

Lawrence Peter

MURPHY'S LAW

If there are two or more ways to
do something, and one of those
ways can result in catastrophe, then
someone will do it.

◆

Edward A. Murphy, Jr.

Do it fast, do it right, do it cheap.
Pick two.

Anonymous

A camel is a horse put together
by a committee.

◆

Anonymous

One may smile, and smile,
and be a villain.

◆

William Shakespeare, *Hamlet*

Don't be afraid of going slowly.
Only be afraid of standing still.

Anonymous

Trust yourself. You know more
than you think you do.

◆

Benjamin Spock

You can gain strength, courage,
and confidence by every experience
in which you really stop to look fear
in the face . . . You must do the thing
which you think you cannot do.

◆

Eleanor Roosevelt

Power can be taken, but not given.
The process of the taking is
empowerment in itself.

◆

Gloria Steinem

When people go to work, they shouldn't have to leave their hearts at home.

◆

Betty Bender

Be nice to people on your way up
because you might meet them
on your way down.

Alexandre Dumas *père*

Investment

At the turn of the twentieth century, two men were walking along the East River waterfront, not far from the headquarters of the New York Stock Exchange. One man pointed to the array of elegant sailing boats tied to the dock and said, "Those yachts belong to the celebrated stockbrokers on Wall Street." The other man looked at him and asked, "Where are all the customers' yachts?"

◆

Fred Schwed, Jr.

Our favorite holding period is forever.

◆

Warren Buffett

It is not how much you make that counts,
but how much money you keep.

◆

Robert Kiyosaki

Make no investments without a
full acquaintance with their nature and
condition; and select such investments
as have intrinsic value.

◆

Benjamin Franklin

Never invest your money in anything
that eats or needs repairing.

Billy Rose

The market is a place set apart where
men may deceive each other.

◆

Diogenes Laertius

Bulls make money. Bears make money.
Pigs get slaughtered.

◆

Anonymous

Business? It's quite simple.
It's other people's money.

◆

Alexandre Dumas *fils*

Sometimes your best investments are
the ones you don't make.

Donald Trump, quoting W. H. Auden

Management

A good manager is a man who isn't worried about his own career but rather the careers of those who work for him. My advice: Don't worry about yourself. Take care of those who work for you and you'll float to greatness on their achievements.

◆

H. S. M. Burns

There is no substitute for accurate
knowledge. Know yourself, know your
business, know your men.

◆

Randall Jacobs

Use the right tool for the job.
Let the tool do the work.
Take care of your tools.

◆

Stanley E. West

Surround yourself with the best
people you can find, delegate authority,
and don't interfere.

◆

Ronald Reagan

Make every decision as if you
owned the whole company.

◆

Robert Townsend

Never mistake activity for achievement.

◆

John Wooden

The ideas that come out of most
brainstorming sessions are usually
superficial, trivial, and not very original.
They are rarely useful. The process,
however, seems to make uncreative people
feel that they are making innovative
contributions and that
others are listening to them.

◆

A. Harvey Block

It is amazing what can be
accomplished when nobody cares
about who gets the credit.

Robert Yates

Compromise is the art of dividing
a cake in such a way that everyone believes
that he has got the biggest piece.

◆

Ludwig Erhard

Behavior in offices often resembles the wild. For example, when a lion is stalking its prey, herd animals are restless and prone to stampede, but after the lion makes its kill, the herd animals soon return to grazing peacefully.

◆

Anonymous

Competition between individuals
sets one against the other and
undermines morale, but competition
between organizations builds morale
and encourages creativity.

◆

George Washington Allston

Avoid mushroom management
(keeping your employees in the dark
and covered in horseshit).

Anonymous

Tell me and I'll forget,
show me and I may remember,
involve me and I'll understand.

◆

Chinese proverb

Surround yourself with skeptics, not true believers who tell you what you want to hear. Demand that your gatekeepers be truth tellers, too, and that they push back whenever they see a lapse in judgment on your part.

◆

David F. D'Alessandro

Any manager who can't get along
with a .400 hitter is crazy.

Joe McCarthy

Business, more than any other occupation,
is a continual dealing with the future;
it is a continual calculation,
an instinctive exercise in foresight.

Henry R. Luce

First-rate people hire
first-rate people;
second-rate people hire
third-rate people.

◆

Leo Rosten

It's not what you pay a man
but what he costs you that counts.

◆

Will Rogers

The budget evolved from a management tool into an obstacle to management.

◆

Frank Carlucci

Marketing

◆

The customer is god.

◆

Japanese proverb

Profit in business comes from repeat customers, customers that boast about your project or service, and that bring friends with them.

◆

W. Edwards Deming

Many a small thing has been made large
by the right kind of advertising.

◆

Mark Twain

Early to bed, early to rise.
Work like hell and advertise.

◆

Ted Turner

UNIQUE SELLING PROPOSITION

- Each advertisement must make a proposition to the consumer.

- The proposition must be one that the competition either cannot or does not offer. It must be unique— either a uniqueness of the brand or a claim not otherwise made in that particular field of advertising.

- The proposition must be so strong that it can move the mass millions.

◆

Rosser Reeves

The consumer isn't a moron.
She is your wife.

◆

David Ogilvy

Anybody can cut prices, but it takes brains
to produce a better article.

◆

P. D. Armour

Success

◆

Trust your hunches. They're usually
based on facts filed away just below
the conscious level.

◆

Dr. Joyce Brothers

Opportunity is missed by most people because it comes dressed in overalls and looks like work.

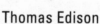

Thomas Edison

There is no security on this earth.
There is only opportunity.

◆

Douglas MacArthur

Whenever you are asked if you can do a job, tell 'em, "Certainly, I can!" Then get busy and find out how to do it.

◆

Theodore Roosevelt

The difference between a successful person and others is not a lack of strength, not a lack of knowledge, but rather a lack of will.

◆

Vince Lombardi

If you want something done, ask a busy person to do it. The more things you do, the more you can do.

◆

Lucille Ball

When I was young I observed that
nine out of ten things I did were failures,
so I did ten times more work.

George Bernard Shaw

I don't measure a man's success by how high he climbs, but how high he bounces when he hits bottom.

◆

George S. Patton

I was told over and over again that I would never be successful, that I was not going to be competitive and the technique was simply not going to work. All I could do was shrug and say, "We'll just have to see."

◆

Dick Fosbury, whose revolutionary high-jumping technique enabled him to win an Olympic gold medal in 1968

People of mediocre ability sometimes achieve outstanding success because they don't know when to quit. Most men succeed because they are determined to.

◆

George E. Allen

Whenever an individual decides
that success has been attained,
progress stops.

◆

Thomas J. Watson, Jr.

Some people believe that holding on
and hanging in there are signs of great
strength. However, there are times when
it takes much more strength to know
when to let go—and then to do it.

◆

Ann Landers

There is nothing so useless as doing
efficiently that which should not
be done at all.

Peter Drucker

It is awfully important to know what
is and what is not your business.

◆

Gertrude Stein

The biggest mistake we could ever make in our lives is to think we work for anybody but ourselves.

◆

Brian Tracy

I have found that being honest is the best technique I can use. Right up front, tell people what you're trying to accomplish and what you're willing to sacrifice to accomplish it.

◆

Lee Iacocca

The secret of life is honesty and
fair dealing . . . If you can fake that,
you've got it made.

◆

Groucho Marx

The essence of success is that it is never necessary to think of a new idea oneself. It is far better to wait until somebody else does it, and then to copy him in every detail, except his mistakes.

◆

Aubrey Menen

A memorandum is written not to inform
the reader, but to protect the writer.

◆

Dean Acheson

Private victories precede public victories.

◆

Stephen R. Covey

One of the symptoms of an approaching
nervous breakdown is the belief that one's
work is terribly important.

◆

Bertrand Russell

Don't be irreplaceable—if you can't be
replaced, you can't be promoted.

◆

Dilbert (Scott Adams)

Conducting your business in a socially responsible way is good business. It means that you can attract better employees and that customers will know what you stand for and like you for it.

◆

M. Anthony Burns

I don't know the key to success,
but the key to failure is trying
to please everybody.

◆

Bill Cosby

It's a poor workman who
blames his tools.

◆

Anonymous

PART II:
SALES TIPS

◆

We are always selling something, all the time. As a consequence, millions of words of advice have been written to help people sell better. Among these millions of words, a few stand out for their clarity, their specificity, and their general application not only to opening an account and closing a sale, but to living a useful and successful life. This is because selling is simply one of many forms of persuasion, and without the ability to persuade others to one's point of view, mankind would still remain in a state of savagery far more primitive than the one we actually exist in today. Accordingly, while this book is designed to offer sales professionals a concise guide to the best that has been thought and said about the fundamentals of selling, the wisdom gathered here can be applied to other human endeavors as well.

This section is divided into four parts. The first is **Motivation**, because no one can sell successfully without proper motivation. One might think that the prospect of financial gains would be enough to motivate any potential salesperson, but in fact, as many of those quoted here emphasize, enthusiasm for what you are selling, and for the process of selling itself, is a prerequisite for success in sales.

The second part deals with **Preparation**. No matter how spontaneous a successful sales presentation may be, it can only benefit from study, practice, and a mastery of the techniques involved in convincing someone to buy what you are offering, whether product, service, or point of view.

The third and largest part deals with **Presenting**. The invaluable advice contained here ranges from philosophy to psychology to the most basic principles of placing your message before a potential customer. Understanding what your customer is looking for (without necessarily even knowing it!) is as important as a firm handshake and steady eye contact.

The final section is on **Service**, because no matter how effective the presentation, retaining a customer's trust *after* a sale is essential if the sales effort is to be judged successful.

The sales tips provided here represent the combined wisdom of some of the greatest sales professionals of all time, together with a sampling of philosophers, poets, and assorted geniuses of all types. We hope that salespeople everywhere will find this to be a helpful guide and an inspiring companion.

Motivation

Believe that you will succeed,
and you will.

◆

Dale Carnegie

Obstacles are necessary for success because in selling, as in all careers of importance, victory comes only after many struggles and countless defeats. Yet each struggle, each defeat, sharpens your skills and strengths, your courage and your endurance, your ability and your confidence and thus each obstacle is a comrade-in-arms forcing you to become better . . . or quit. Each rebuff is an opportunity to move forward; turn away from them, avoid them, and you throw away your future.

◆

Og Mandino

The most important thing in life is
not to capitalize on your successes—any
fool can do that. The really important thing
is to profit from your mistakes.

◆

William Bolitho

Motivation is a fire from within.
If someone else tries to light
that fire under you, chances are it
will burn very briefly.

◆

Stephen R. Covey

Find a job you love and you will never
have to work a day in your life.

◆

Confucius

Recently, I heard the top salesperson of an organization make the statement, "I can't endorse this product any longer." A visiting consultant replied, "Then it's time for you to go find a product or service you can endorse." Within one week, the Number 1 salesperson for that organization left the company. Was that the right choice? Yes. When you don't believe in your product or service, you're being dishonest with your prospects and customers when you present the benefits and value of what you sell to them. Talk about internal turmoil! If you don't believe in your product or service, and don't have faith that it will accomplish what you say it will— then "it's time for you to go."

◆

Byron White

I will! I am! I can! I will actualize
my dream. I will press ahead. I will
settle down and see it through. I
will solve the problems. I will pay the
price. I will never walk away from my
dream until I see my dream walk away:
Alert! Alive! Achieved!

◆

Robert Schuller

On any given Monday I am one
sale closer and one idea away
from being a millionaire.

◆

Larry D. Turner

You've got to be success minded. You've got to feel that things are coming your way when you're out selling; otherwise, you won't be able to sell anything.

◆

Curtis Carlson

Always bear in mind that our own
resolution to succeed is more important
than any other one thing.

◆

Abraham Lincoln

The essential element in personal magnetism is a consuming sincerity—an overwhelming faith in the importance of the work one has to do.

Bruce Barton

Being sincere is the easiest part of selling.
It's simply a matter of caring about your
customer and believing in what you sell.
If you don't feel this way, my advice to you
is to seek other employment or find
a product to sell that you believe in.

◆

Joe Girard

Motivation is the art of getting
people to do what you want them to do
because they want to do it.

◆

Dwight D. Eisenhower

Two shoe salesmen found themselves in a rustic part of Africa. The first salesman wired back to his head office: "There is no prospect of sales. No one here wears shoes!" The other salesman wired: "No one wears shoes here. We can dominate the market. Send all possible stock."

◆

Akio Morita

Fall down seven times. Stand up eight.

◆

Japanese proverb

There are no traffic jams
along the extra mile.

◆

Roger Staubach

People buy for their own reasons,
not for yours.

◆

Stephen E. Heiman

I once heard a car salesman say,
"I peddle metal." Well, I disagree.
To the extent I do "peddle" anything,
I sell helpfulness and solutions. That to
me is the heart of the sales experience.
That's what a good salesperson really
does—identifies a need and fills it.

◆

Marion Luna Brem

When you have a passion
for your product, selling is the natural
by-product of sharing the love.

Kae Groshong

A salesman minus enthusiasm
is just a clerk.

◆

Harry F. Banks

Sincerity is the biggest part of selling anything, I found out—including salvation. And I was sure that when I was selling Fuller brushes that those were the greatest brushes in the whole world.

◆

Billy Graham

There's nothing greater in the world than when somebody on the team does something good, and everybody gathers around to pat him on the back.

◆

Billy Martin

Your big opportunity may be right
where you are now.

◆

Napoleon Hill

Preparation

◆

One important key to success is
self-confidence. An important key
to self-confidence is preparation.

Arthur Ashe

When you're prepared, you're more confident. When you have a strategy, you're more comfortable.

Fred Couples

By failing to prepare, you are
preparing to fail.
◆

Benjamin Franklin

We are what we repeatedly do.
Excellence, then, is not an act,
but a habit.

Aristotle

Let your hook be always cast;
in the pool where you least expect it,
there will be a fish.

Ovid

Internalize the Golden Rule of sales that says, "All things being equal, people will do business with, and refer business to, those people they know, like, and trust."

◆

Bob Burg

Pack your todays with effort
—extra effort.

◆

Thomas J. Watson

Know your product.
See a lot of people.
Ask all to buy.
Use common sense.

◆

Arthur H. "Red" Motley

Many a small thing has been made large
by the right kind of advertising.

◆

Mark Twain

I am the world's worst salesman,
therefore, I must make it easy
for people to buy.

◆

F. W. Woolworth

The single most important thing you can do for sweaty palms is rehearse. The second most important thing you can do for sweaty palms is rehearse. Guess what the third thing is?

◆

David Peoples

Ralph Waldo Emerson was quoted as saying, if a man can make a better mousetrap than his neighbor, the world will make a beaten path to his door. His actual statement was written in a journal as follows: "If a man has good corn, or wood, or boards, or pigs to sell, or can make better chairs or knives, crucibles or church organs than anybody else, you will find a broad hard-beaten road to his house, though it be in the woods."

The mousetrap quote was written by an ad guy, Elbert Hubbard, who attributed it to Emerson twenty-eight years after Emerson died! Emerson had the great thought, but it took a good copywriter to make it a memorable thought . . . You may have great products and services, but unless you can communicate well, you're doomed.

◆

Matt Michel

Plan your progress carefully;
hour-by-hour, day-by-day,
month-by-month. Organized activity
and maintained enthusiasm are the
wellsprings of your power.

◆

Paul J. Meyer

Don't start your day until you have it
finished on paper first.

◆

Jim Rohn

When leaving a message with a receptionist, ask for a specific time your prospect will be available to speak with you and be sure to call at that time. Learn the receptionist's name, and address him by name every time you call the prospect. Remember to be courteous to everyone you speak to, as each person is a gatekeeper to your prospect.

◆

Ron Coxsom

If you're making telemarketing calls and having trouble getting past the receptionist, then the next time you call that company go up or down one number on the last digit of the general phone number to reach someone else who might be more helpful. Every time I've tried it people other than the receptionist have been more than helpful.

◆

Todd Benadum

There's no magic to it, and you don't need a lot of natural talent. What you need is a disciplined, organized approach to selling. If you have that, you'll outperform the great salesman who doesn't understand the process every time. Selling can definitely be learned.

◆

Steve Bostic

The business handshake is an
essential selling technique to make
a lasting impression. The first move you
make when meeting your prospective
client is to put out your hand. There isn't
a businessperson anywhere who can't tell
you that the good business handshake
should be a firm one. Yet time and again
people offer a limp hand to the client.
To have a good business handshake,
position your hand to make complete
contact with the other person's hand. Once
you've connected, close your thumb over
the back of the other person's hand and give
a slight squeeze. You'll have the beginning
of a strong business relationship.

◆

Lydia Ramsey

In the late 1980s, I was a spectacularly unsuccessful burglar-alarm salesman, consistently ranking dead last in weekly sales. As an avid golfer since grade school, I fared better on the back nine and still competed as a part-time pro. During a 1988 game, I told my partner precisely how I planned to get on the 18th green: hit the ball two hundred yards, curve it forty yards from left to right, and drop it about six feet from the hole. Then I did exactly that.

My astonished colleague demanded to know my secret. I said, "I practiced for years. I trained. I had in my mind's eye what I was trying to do." And that's when it hit me: That's how the great salesmen do it. They practice. They train. I realized that if I worked as hard at selling as I did at golf, I'd never look back. And I never have.

◆

Dave Hegan

Every sale has five basic obstacles:
no need, no money, no hurry,
no desire, no trust.

◆

Zig Ziglar

It's simple: Sell to people who want your product; ignore those who don't. I spent years trying to get people to buy into Macintosh. We were selling a dream of how the world might become a better place. That kind of selling requires a different mind-set from that of trying to meet a quota. Some people got it in thirty seconds. Others didn't get it and never would. It took me a while to learn that you can't convert atheists. You can't sell oil to Arabs, or refrigerators to Eskimos. Don't even try.

◆

Guy Kawasaki

Clean out your prospect funnel. Put your current prospects through a sieve. The biggest mistake salespeople make is they call on the same useless prospects over and over. If you have not been able to get anywhere with a specific group of prospects, move on and find new prospects. Being persistent is good. However, if you are spending too much time on fruitless leads you will just burn out. After a shepherd's herd has eaten all the grass in a specific pasture he knows it's time to move on to a new pasture. If he does not move on his sheep will starve. Move on if you are not getting anywhere with old prospects and come back at a later date.

◆

Larry Duca

You can learn a lot about sales and marketing from studying insects. The two insects I like to watch most are bumblebees and spiders. A bumblebee flies as much as fifty miles from home to pollinate a really choice flower "prospect." Here comes that big bee. There goes that big bee. He really, really racks up the frequent flier miles . . . know what we mean? The spider, on the other hand, puts less emphasis on "direct sales" and relies more on studying the best principles of sales and marketing. He does market research and determines that if he locates his web in an area of high traffic flow, he will snare more than his share of "customers" without having to pack as little as a toothbrush for those tiresome road trips. Strategic marketing beats road selling every time. Who says you can't make a living sitting in one place? Couch potatoes, rejoice . . . but tend to your "netting."

◆

Stan Rosenzweig

When I prepare for a sales presentation, I try to think like my client and like my competitor. I try to pinpoint every objection that either of them could make to my presentation. I write these objections down, and then I figure out a way to respond to each one in three lines or less. I've given these "scripts" to sales reps, who then used them in their presentations. It's staggering how even the most boring sales rep can become a great salesperson simply by learning to convey a few simple points. If you can move a customer so that he or she can't argue against your point, then you've won.

◆

Mark Jarvis

Are you born a good salesperson or is the art of selling a natural skill? I'm not sure I knew the answer myself until I was fortunate enough to meet the greatest salesman who ever lived. It was a fellow named Ben Feldman. You probably haven't heard of him either, but you should have. In 1979, while I was with the New York Life Insurance Company, Ben led the industry in sales. That is, all the insurance companies, not just mine. Actually, it is unfair to say he led the industry—he dominated it. The top nine agents were all fairly close to each other. Ben Feldman tripled the next closest competitor. I had never seen a picture of Ben, but I imagined what he looked like. Outgoing, tall, aggressive, big booming voice. Really, I guess I saw him as a collection of every stereotype I had been led to believe was necessary to be an effective salesperson. One day I had the rare pleasure of meeting this man, and, in a way, he changed my life. Ben Feldman stood about five foot three, somewhat overweight, had hair a little like Larry from the Three Stooges, and spoke with a heavy lisp. Not quite what I had expected. Within seconds, however, I was drawn to the unique style that Ben Feldman possessed. He had none of the more conventional strengths that we associate with his kind of success, yet he remained true to his style, made what he had his strengths, and was dominant in his field.

It was then and there I learned the most valuable lesson I would ever receive in my life regarding our own personal style: I could not be Ben Feldman; I could, however, focus on his technique or process and continue to ask myself, "How can I do that so it sounds like Rob Jolles? What is my personal style?" Rob's strengths aren't Ben's strengths, but then again, Ben's aren't Rob's either . . .

Can anybody sell? Absolutely! The key is to separate style from technique . . . In the summer of 1994 Ben Feldman passed away but not without leaving us a few final gifts . . . He taught us all that if you commit to your own personal style and do not worry about anyone else's strengths or style, you can become as great as you want to be.

◆

Robert L. Jolles

Presenting

Speak clearly, if you speak at all;
carve every word before you let it fall.

◆

Oliver Wendell Holmes

Remember, your customers don't buy
your product. They buy you. If they
buy you, they will sell your product
for you. I treat my potential customers
as I would treat a stranger whom
I wanted to be my friend.

◆

Alfred E. Lyon

If I can tell you one thing: Remember that it's not what and how you *sell* something that's important, it's what and how your customer wishes to *buy* that's important.

◆

Freeman Gosden

Sell cheap and tell the truth.

◆

Rose Blumkin

As you travel down life's highway . . .
whatever be your goal, you
cannot sell a doughnut without
acknowledging the hole.

◆

Harold J. Shayler

No one can remember more
than three points.

◆

Philip Crosby

Customers usually buy on impulse, not logic. They base their buying decision on how they feel about your product or service. Get them excited about using your product or service and you'll increase your sales.

◆

Bob Leduc

The spectator-buyer is meant to envy herself as she will become if she buys the product. She is meant to imagine herself transformed by the product into an object of envy for others, an envy which will then justify her loving herself. One could put this another way: The publicity image steals her love of herself as she is, and offers it back to her for the price of the product.

◆

John Berger

Sell to people who want what you have. Figure out who those people are by asking them. Ask as many questions as you need to see if they are good prospects. Be radically honest. Do not fudge in order to pique people's interest. If there is no obvious match, cut them loose—quickly.

◆

Jacques Werth

If a product isn't selling, I want to get it out of there because it's taking up space that can be devoted to another part of my line that moves. Besides, having a product languish on the shelves doesn't do much for our image.

◆

Norman Melnick

People don't like to be sold,
but they love to buy.

◆

Jeffrey Gitomer

It is most important in this world to be pushing; it is fatal to seem so.

◆

Benjamin Jowett

The marksman hitteth the target partly by pulling, partly by letting go. The boatsman reacheth the landing partly by pulling, partly by letting go.

◆

Egyptian proverb

Every additional message causes an earlier one to be forgotten. What do you want the audience to hear? Say it clearly and with confidence . . . then shut up.

◆

Adrian Savage

Most people think "selling" is the same as "talking." But the most effective salespeople know that listening is the most important part of their job.

◆

Roy Bartell

When people talk, listen completely.
Most people never listen.

◆

Ernest Hemingway

Make sure you have finished speaking
before your audience has finished listening.

◆

Dorothy Sarnoff

If you want to eliminate sales resistance, treat your prospects the way you'd like to be treated—as peers.

◆

Gill E. Wagner

Traditional selling is based on the product or service sale, and yet until buyers know how decisions and new purchases will affect their culture they will delay their decisions.

◆

Sharon Drew Morgen

A mediocre salesman tells. A good salesman explains. A superior salesman demonstrates. Great salesmen inspire buyers to see the benefits as their own.

Carolyn Shamis

A smart salesperson listens
to emotions, not facts.

◆

Anonymous

You never give less attention to the female than to the man. Just because she's not buying doesn't mean she can't break the sale.

Victoria Gallegos

If I say it, they can doubt me.
If they say it, it's true.

◆

Tom Hopkins

When people laugh at your jokes,
they are involuntarily agreeing
with your message.

Jim Richardson

One of the keys needed to sell is entertainment; the more you entertain your prospect the greater your chance of creating a personal contact. This does not mean going to the pub or girly bars. This means during your presentation, being interesting and animated.

◆

David Beacham

At the age of three, we all possessed
three important skills to make the sale:
persistence, creativity, and the ability
to ask one question after another.

◆

Dirk Zeller

"No" never means "No"
—it just means "Not now."

◆

Mark Bozzini

Call the bald man "Boy"; make the sage thy toy; greet the youth with solemn face; praise the fat man for his grace.

Helen Rowland

One of the best pieces of advice I ever received was from an old, grizzled salesman who'd seen it all. "Just *sell* the damn thing," he'd say. "Stop trying to be fancy."

◆

John Carlton

The best way to sell to anyone is to tell it like it is—which sounds simple but apparently isn't. For instance, look at the boys in Detroit. I'm always amazed by how they sell cars. Instead of grounding their sales pitch in the benefits of their cars, they talk about lifestyle and being cool—or about limited-slip differential and rack-and-pinion steering. No one knows what those things mean! People know when they're being duped. So the best way to sell to them is not to try to dupe them.

◆

Tom Scott

Imagine you are so sick that the doctor had to make a house call. Then when the doctor walked in your house, he started by telling you that you should buy some pills, an extra shot that was on sale that week, some brand X bandages that would reduce healing time by 57 percent, and some life insurance from his brother . . . I would not ask that doctor to come back, yet many sales reps have a similar approach and wonder why customers don't buy from them.

When giving a sales presentation, identify what the prospect's headache is, what keeps him up at night. Once you have identified at least three problem areas of concern, then show your aspirin (solution) that will take care of that headache.

◆

Martien Eerhart

Only after you've correctly assessed the needs of your prospect do you mention anything about what you're offering. I knew a guy who pitched a mannequin (I'm not kidding)! He was so stuck in his own automated, habitual mode, he never bothered to notice that his prospect wasn't breathing. Don't get caught in this trap. Know whom you're speaking with before figuring out what it is you want to say.

◆

Len Foley

I was eleven years old, selling soap door to door to earn my way to YMCA camp. I'd say, "Hello, my name is Brian Tracy. I'm selling Rosamel beauty soap. Would you like to buy a box?" People would say, "No, don't need it, don't want it, can't afford it," etc. I was very frustrated—until I rephrased my presentation: "I'm selling Rosamel beauty soap, but it's strictly for beautiful women." People who had been completely uninterested would say, "Well, that's not for me. It wouldn't help me. How much is it?" I started selling the soap like hot cakes.

◆

Brian Tracy

Engage your audience by telling stories. Begin the story even before doing introductions and use this to get their attention and take full control. What kind of story should you tell? The best stories are ones that the prospect can relate to.

Tell a story about one of your customers who had a big problem and how they solved it by doing business with you. Make the story engaging by describing it in vivid emotional detail—who was affected by the problem, how was it impacting them, how did they feel, and how did the solution change all of this?

Take your feature benefit points and weave them into the story. They will have ten times the impact and will be remembered when delivered this way.

◆

Shamus Brown

Make eye contact, especially when you are stressing the key reason for the conversation. Eye contact is a visual handshake; it is the way you connect nonverbally with the other person. Don't stare at the person, but regularly connect with your eyes. When you look at the person you are saying, "Pay attention to me."

◆

Stephen Boyd

At its conclusion, a good presentation summarizes the key themes in a way that makes the audience feel like they just got off the Jungle Cruise at Disneyland. They learned some stuff, had an enjoyable ride with a few surprises along the way—and knew exactly where they were when the ride was over.

◆

Jim Endicott

A-B-C. A-always, B-be, C-closing.
Always be closing! Always be closing!!
A-I-D-A.
Attention, interest, decision, action.

◆

David Mamet

Service

There is tremendous value in being a resource for your client. If you can help them to succeed then they are more likely to help you succeed.

◆

Lee Ann Obringer

Quality isn't something that can be argued into an article or promised into it. It must be put there. If it isn't put there, the finest sales talk in the world won't act as a substitute.

◆

C. G. Campbell

Being on par in terms of price and quality only gets you into the game. Service wins the game.

♦

Tony Alessandra

Make a customer, not a sale.

◆

Katherine Barchetti

It is not your customers' job to remember you. It is your obligation and responsibility to make sure they don't have the chance to forget you.

◆

Patricia Frip

Neglected customers never buy;
they just fade away.

◆

Elmer G. Leterman

The only way to know how
customers see your business is to
look at it through their eyes.

◆

Daniel R. Scroggin

To satisfy our customers' needs,
we'll give them what they want,
not what we want to give them.

Steve James

Here is a simple but powerful rule—
always give people more
than what they expect to get.

◆

Nelson Boswell

Rule #1: The customer is always right!
Rule #2: If the customer is wrong,
reread Rule #1.

Stew Leonard

Sell practical, tested merchandise
at a reasonable profit, treat your customers
like human beings—
and they will always come back.

L.L. Bean

Losers make promises they often
break. Winners make commitments
they always keep.

◆

Denis Waitley

Always serve too much hot fudge sauce on hot fudge sundaes. It makes people overjoyed, and puts them in your debt.

◆

Judith Olney

Always do more than is required of you.

◆

George S. Patton

PART III:
LEADERSHIP PRINCIPLES

◆

*Leadership is a matter of intelligence, trustworthiness,
humaneness, courage, and discipline . . . Reliance
on **intelligence** alone results in rebelliousness.
Exercise of **humaneness** alone results in weakness.
Fixation on **trust** results in folly. Dependence on the
strength of **courage** results in violence. Excessive
discipline and sternness in command result in cruelty.
When one has all five virtues together, each appropriate
to its function, then one can be a leader.*

— Sun Tzu

Sun Tzu's *Art of War* originally was intended to be read as a work
of military strategy and philosophy. Yet even today, more than 2,000
years later, Sun Tzu's description of the traits that characterize a successful
leader is valid in any arena—war, politics, business, and any endeavor that
requires the ability to inspire and mobilize the efforts of a group in the
service of a common goal.

Taking Sun Tzu's categories as a point of departure, this section of
the book is divided into five parts, each one containing twenty quotations
that offer different perspectives on the requirements of leadership. The
attentive reader will note that some of the principles seem to comment on
others in different sections; for example, in the section on trustworthiness,
Douglas McArthur is quoted as saying "Never give an order that can't
be obeyed"; while in the section on discipline, these words of Sophocles
appear: "What you cannot enforce, do not command." Almost the same
sentiment, but not quite: Sophocles focuses on the leader, and McArthur

on the led. It's in the conjunction of similar and even sometimes apparently conflicting principles that a three-dimensional image of the leader is intended to emerge.

What kind of person is the theoretical ideal leader? The ideal leader has the intelligence to understand the subtleties and complexity of the leadership role: It is not sufficient to bear the title and hold the authority of a leader to function as one. The very concept of leadership is subjective, which is why so many different varieties and degrees of leadership are evident in society and in business. The perfect leader understands what it means to lead, and to be led.

The ideal leader is aware of the mutual responsibility of the leader and the led: Each relies on and supports the other. A leader without a sense of humanity is only a leader by virtue of superior power, while a great leader inspires more by force of character and principle than by fear and intimidation.

A successful leader is courageous, and not simply in the physical sense. Many decisions must be made in solitude, even when the leader has numerous counselors. The perfect leader is one who willingly takes on the responsibility for advancing or retreating, and accepts the consequences. If the leader is not seen to have the courage required to act on behalf of all, the leader will lose the confidence of the group, and ultimately the position of leadership itself. Finally, the perfect leader must impose discipline, in the classic sense of teaching followers the correct path. Discipline is not simply exercising control and punishing those who fail to obey instructions. Discipline is guidance, structure, training; without it, no one can lead effectively.

Sun Tzu pointed out that each of the qualities he mentions as essential for leadership can lead to excess and abuse. It is only by balancing the proportions of these qualities that the leader can attain maximum effectiveness. We hope that in reading and contemplating the principles in this book, you will find your own personal path to leadership.

Intelligence

Many people have ideas on how others should change; few people have ideas on how they should change.

Leo Tolstoy

It's amazing how many cares
disappear when you decide not to be
something, but to be someone.
◆

Coco Chanel

The only real training for
leadership is leadership.

◆

Anthony Jay

The ultimate leader is one who is
willing to develop people to the point
that they surpass him or her in
knowledge and ability.

◆

Fred A. Manske

A genuine leader is not a searcher for consensus but a molder of consensus.

◆

Martin Luther King, Jr.

Do not go where the path may lead.
Go instead where there is
no path and leave a trail.

◆

Ralph Waldo Emerson

Forethought and prudence are the
proper qualities of a leader.

◆

Tacitus

A true leader always keeps an element
of surprise up his sleeve, which
others cannot grasp but which keeps his
public excited and breathless.

◆

Charles deGaulle

Those who know how to win are more numerous than those who know how to make proper use of their victories.

Polybius

If a man does not know to what port he is steering, no wind is favorable to him.

◆

Seneca

Leadership Principles

I used to think that running an organization was equivalent to conducting a symphony orchestra. But I don't think that's quite it; it's more like jazz. There is more improvisation.

◆

Warren Bennis

The first method for estimating the intelligence of a ruler is to look at the men he has around him.

Niccolo Machiavelli

The chief executive who knows his strengths and weaknesses as a leader is likely to be far more effective than the one who remains blind to them. He also is on the road to humility—that priceless attitude of openness to life that can help a manager to absorb mistakes, failures, or personal shortcomings.

◆

John Adair

Management is efficiency in
climbing the ladder of success;
leadership determines whether the
ladder is leaning against the right wall.
◆

Stephen R. Covey

One of the tests of leadership is
to recognize a problem before it
becomes an emergency.

Arnold Glasow

There's nothing more demoralizing
than a leader who can't clearly articulate
why we're doing what we're doing.

◆

James Kouzes and Barry Posner

There are no mistakes so great
as that of being always right.

◆

Samuel Butler

You can use all the quantitative data you can get, but you still have to distrust it and use your own intelligence and judgment.

◆

Alvin Toffler

A leader is one who sees more than others see, who sees farther than others see, and who sees before others see.

Leroy Eimes

Great spirits have always found violent opposition from mediocrities. The latter cannot understand it when a man does not thoughtlessly submit to hereditary prejudices but honestly and courageously uses his intelligence.

◆

Albert Einstein

Trustworthiness

We must become the change
we want to see.

Mahatma Gandhi

A good leader can't get too
far ahead of his followers.

◆

Franklin D. Roosevelt

Never give an order that can't be obeyed.

◆

Douglas MacArthur

I cannot trust a man to control others
who cannot control himself.

Robert E. Lee

No man is wise enough by himself.

◆

Plautus

No man will make a great leader who
wants to do it all himself, or to get
all the credit for doing it.

Andrew Carnegie

You don't have to hold a position
in order to be a leader.

◆

Anthony D'Angelo

I have yet to find the man, however exalted his station, who did not do better work and put forth greater effort under a spirit of criticism.

◆

Charles Schwab

Never hire or promote in your own image. It is foolish to replicate your strength and idiotic to replicate your weakness. It is essential to employ, trust, and reward those whose perspective, ability, and judgment are radically different from yours. It is also rare, for it requires uncommon humility, tolerance, and wisdom.

◆

Dee W. Hock

Help others get ahead. You will
always stand taller with someone
else on your shoulders.

Bob Moawad

The leaders who work most effectively, it seems to me, never say "I." And that's not because they have trained themselves not to say "I." They don't think "I." They think "we"; they think "team." They understand their job to be to make the team function. They accept responsibility and don't sidestep it, but "we" gets the credit . . . This is what creates trust, what enables you to get the task done.

◆

Peter F. Drucker

It is important that an aim never be defined in terms of activity or methods. It must always relate directly to how life is better for everyone . . . The aim of the system must be clear to everyone in the system. The aim must include plans for the future. The aim is a value judgment.

◆

W. Edwards Deming

Treat people as if they were what they
ought to be and you help them to become
what they are capable of being.

◆

Johann Wolfgang von Goethe

One measure of leadership is the caliber
of people who choose to follow you.

◆

Dennis A. Peer

A true leader has to have a genuine open-door policy so that his people are not afraid to approach him for any reason.

◆

Harold Geneen

Leadership is getting people to work for
you when they are not obligated.

◆

Fred Smith

A leader leads by example,
whether he intends to or not.

◆

Anonymous

Delegating work works, provided
the one delegating works too.

◆

Robert Half

Leaders are dealers in hope.

Napoleon

The first responsibility of a leader is to define reality. The last is to say "thank you." In between, the leader is servant.

◆

Max DePree

Humaneness

The man whose authority is
recent is always stern.

◆

Aeschylus

Be kind, for everyone you meet
is fighting a hard battle.

Plato

To lead people, walk beside them . . .
As for the best leaders, the people
do not notice their existence. The next
best, the people honor and praise.
The next, the people fear; and the next,
the people hate . . .When the best leader's
work is done the people say,
"We did it ourselves!"

◆

Lao-tse

You do not lead by hitting people over the head—that's assault, not leadership.

◆

Dwight D. Eisenhower

Leadership is a combination of strategy and character. If you must be without one, be without the strategy.

H. Norman Schwarzkopf

Leadership is solving problems. The day soldiers stop bringing you their problems is the day you have stopped leading them. They have either lost confidence that you can help or concluded you do not care. Either case is a failure of leadership.

◆

Karl Popper

He makes a great mistake, who supposes that authority is firmer or better established when it is founded by force than that which is welded by affection.

◆

Terence

Lead and inspire people. Don't try to manage and manipulate people. Inventories can be managed but people must be led.

◆

Ross Perot

There go my people. I must find out
where they are going so I can lead them.

◆

Alexandre Auguste Ledru-Rollin

People ask the difference between a
leader and a boss . . . The leader leads,
and the boss drives.

◆

Theodore Roosevelt

The boss drives his men; the leader coaches them. The boss depends upon authority; the leader on good will. The boss inspires fear; the leader inspires enthusiasm. The boss says "I"; the leader "we." The boss fixes the blame for the breakdown; the leader fixes the breakdown. The boss says "go"; the leader says "let's go!"

◆

Gordon Selfridge

The highest proof of virtue is to possess boundless power without abusing it.

◆

Thomas Babington Macaulay

Do you wish to rise? Begin by descending. You plan a tower that will pierce the clouds? Lay first the foundation of humility.

◆

St. Augustine

In order to make a fire burn, you fan the live coals. In order to keep your organization fired up, it's imperative that you find and motivate the leaders or potential leaders in your organization regardless of how far down the line they might be.

◆

Dexter Yager

Knowledge alone is not enough to get desired results. You must have the more elusive ability to teach and to motivate. This defines a leader; if you can't teach and you can't motivate, you can't lead.

◆

John Wooden

Leaders focus on the soft stuff.
People. Values. Character. Commitment.
A cause. All of the stuff that was
supposed to be too goo-goo to count in
business. Yet it's the stuff that real leaders
take care of first. And forever. That's why
leadership is an art, not a science.

◆

Tom Peters

Nobody rises to low expectations.

◆

Calvin Lloyd

The leader has to be practical and a realist, yet must talk the language of the visionary and the idealist.

Eric Hoffer

Leaders must be close enough
to relate to others, but far enough
ahead to motivate them.

John Maxwell

If I have seen further, it is by standing
on the shoulders of giants.

◆

Isaac Newton

Courage

◆

Abraham Lincoln did not go to
Gettysburg having commissioned a
poll to find out what would sell in
Gettysburg. There were no people with
percentages for him, cautioning him
about this group or that group or what they
found in exit polls a year earlier. When will
we have the courage of Lincoln?

◆

Robert Coles

You've got to jump off cliffs all the time
and build your wings on the way down.

◆

Ray Bradbury

The trouble is, if you don't risk
anything, you risk even more.

◆

Erica Jong

In matters of style, swim with the current;
in matters of principle, stand like a rock.

◆

Thomas Jefferson

Not the cry, but the flight of the wild duck,
leads the flock to fly and follow.

◆

Chinese proverb

Leadership is action, not position.

◆

Donald H. McGannon

Self-assurance is two-thirds of success.

◆

Gaelic proverb

A brave captain is as a root, out of which, as branches, the courage of his soldiers doth spring.

◆

Sir Philip Sidney

If the leader is filled with high ambition
and if he pursues his aims with audacity
and strength of will, he will reach them in
spite of all obstacles.

◆

Karl von Clausewitz

The charismatic leader gains and
maintains authority solely by proving
his strength in life.

Max Weber

Anyone can hold the helm
when the sea is calm.

◆

Pubilius Syrus

It's hard to lead a cavalry charge if you think you look funny on a horse.

Adlai Stevenson

The only way around is through.

Robert Frost

An army of sheep led by a lion would
defeat an army of lions led by a sheep.

◆

Arab proverb

A leader must have the courage to
act against an expert's advice.

◆

James Callaghan

"Safety first" has been the motto of the human race for half a million years; but it has never been the motto of leaders. A leader must face danger. He must take the risk and the blame, and the brunt of the storm.

◆

Herbert N. Casson

If it's a good idea, go ahead and do it.
It is much easier to apologize than it
is to get permission.

◆

Grace Hopper

Don't be afraid to take a big step
when one is indicated. You can't cross
a chasm in two small steps.

◆

David Lloyd George

Most companies don't die because they are wrong; most die because they don't commit themsleves . . . You have to have a strong leader setting a direction. And it doesn't even have to be the best direction—just a strong, clear one.

◆

Andy Grove

Leaders are visionaries with a poorly developed sense of fear and no concept of the odds against them.

◆

Dr. Robert Jarvik

Discipline

◆

Mountaintops inspire leaders
but valleys mature them.

◆

Winston Churchill

All men can stand adversity,
but if you want to test a man's character,
give him power.

◆

Abraham Lincoln

It is not fair to ask of others what you
are unwilling to do yourself.

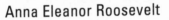

Anna Eleanor Roosevelt

Example is leadership.

◆

Albert Schweitzer

What you cannot enforce,
do not command.

◆

Sophocles

Half of the harm that is done in this world is due to people who want to feel important . . . They do not mean to do harm . . . They are absorbed in the endless struggle to think well of themselves.

◆

T. S. Eliot

Be willing to make decisions. That's the most important quality in a good leader. Don't fall victim to what I call the "ready-aim-aim-aim syndrome." You must be willing to fire.

◆

George S. Patton

The speed of the leader
determines the rate of the pack.

◆

D. Wayne Lukas

The spirited horse, which will try
to win the race of its own accord,
will run even faster if encouraged.

Ovid

A community is like a ship: Everyone ought to be prepared to take the helm.

◆

Henrik Ibsen

For if the trumpet give an uncertain sound, who shall prepare himself to the battle?

◆

St. Paul

Have patience. All things are difficult
before they become easy.

◆

Saadi Shirazi

It is always easier to dismiss a man
than it is to train him. No great leader ever
built a reputation on firing people. Many
have built a reputation on developing them.

◆

Anonymous

I am a man of fixed and unbending
principles, the first of which is to be
flexible at all times.

◆

Everett Dirksen

To be a leader of men,
one must turn one's back on men.

◆

Havelock Ellis

Leadership is a matter of having
people look at you and gain confidence,
seeing how you react. If you're in control,
they're in control.

♦

Tom Landry

In simplest terms, a leader is one
who knows where he wants to go,
and gets up, and goes.

◆

John Erskine

Leadership consists not in degrees
of technique but in traits of character; it
requires moral rather than athletic
or intellectual effort, and it imposes
on both leader and follower alike the
burdens of self-restraint.

◆

Lewis H. Lapham

With great power,
comes great responsibility.

◆

Stan Lee

And when we think we lead,
we are most led.

Lord Byron